MAINE

A Portrait

MAINE

A Portrait

by Lucian Niemeyer

Down East Books / Camden, Maine

Dedicated to Eliot Porter—
the master who showed me the way

Copyright © 2006 by Lucian Niemeyer
All rights reserved.

Map of Maine (p.10) copyright © 2005 by Mike Reagan

The excerpt beginning on page 21 is from *The Edge of the Sea* by Rachel L. Carson
Copyright © 1955 by Rachel L. Carson
Reprinted by permission of Frances Collin, Literary Agent

The excerpt beginning on page 71 is from *My Neck of the Woods* and *We Took to the Woods*
by Louise Dickinson Rich
My Neck of the Woods copyright © 1950 by Louise Dickinson Rich
We Took to the Woods copyright © 1942 by Louise Dickinson Rich
Reprinted by permission of Dinah Clark and Rufus Rich

Printed in China

ISBN 0-89272-697-0

Down East Books
www.nbnbooks.com

Front jacket photograph: The shoreline at Swans Island
Back jacket photograph: Moosehead Lake at Rockwood
Frontispiece: Bar Harbor from Cadillac Mountain

Library of Congress Control Number: 2005938655

Contents

Preface	7
Introduction	11
The Coast	13
from *The Edge of the Sea*—Rachel Carson	21
The Great North Woods	69
from *My Neck of the Woods* and *We Took to the Woods* —Louise Dickinson Rich	71
Afterword	97

Ocean waves at Schoodic Point

Preface

Winter at Bass Harbor Head lighthouse

Facing page: Razorbill auks nest on many of Maine's islands

In 1955, my father gave me an old Leica, and in the 1960s, I grew to love photography and began to photograph as a continuing avocation. I also loved nature, and in particular, Eliot Porter's interpretation of the outdoors. The early Sierra Club books by this consummate master, *Summer Island* and *Galapagos*, were revelations of wonder in which he explored corners of the natural order not often noticed by the layman.

In the late 1960s, I began to collect Eliot Porter's books and referred to them often as *the* standard of excellence. I was in awe of them. Unlike most popular photographers at the time who presented their skills in black and white, and created self-printed photographic images that established photography as an art form, Mr. Porter used early Kodak color film. Not only was color printing quite unstable, it was also unsuitable for museum use because the prints faded in a few short years. The Sierra Club books were an exception. They were printed with great skill and color faithfulness; and they were archival. They are as up-to-date today as when they were first printed. For this, David Brower, former Director of the Sierra Club, should be proud. Eventually, the development of the Kodak dye transfer print process provided a high degree of permanence that both the art itself and museums needed. Eliot Porter welcomed this breakthrough, which helped open the door for the acceptance of color photography as art.

In the field, Eliot Porter used a large format view camera. Though heavy and cumbersome to manipulate, he was able to achieve a large photographic image. His attention to detail in his final presentation was legendary, and this image size provided him easy access to preview and edit. He never failed to produce "a good story" in his work.

Mr. Porter began his photographic profession late in his life (in his late thirties), all the more remarkable for the volume of work that he accomplished in his career. Opening the door for color photography as a legitimate art form and twenty-seven books are the result of his pioneering effort in color photography. I should note that I, too, started my formal photographic career later in my life; I was in my fifties.

As he has been for my previous books, Eliot Porter is the inspiration behind *Maine: A Portrait*. In 1998, I was between books and decided to take a walk in Mr. Porter's footsteps to see his view of Maine. A few trips later, my wife Joan and I decided that a book of Maine photographs should be the result. In the two years that we have worked on this book, we have come to better appreciate Eliot Porter's view of Maine and his body of work.

For my study of Maine, some thirty years later, I used Leica 35mm single lens reflex cameras with neutrally color-balanced films, and no filters or fill-in light. Like Mr. Porter, I did not enhance or alter my images in any way, even though, with some nature shots, I did use a longer lens (400mm). Usually, I shot with a 60mm or 100mm Leica macro lens. This smaller and lighter equipment and faster, improved films afforded me a far greater flexibility and range for shooting than Mr. Porter could attain. The extensive use of a car also allowed me to traverse Maine easily and comfortably. I have used these newfound abilities to expand the scope of this study with more varied subjects and locations, which has, ultimately, allowed me to tell my story.

I have included a revealing and elegant essay from Rachel Carson's book *Edge of the Sea* for its sublime essence of the Maine coast. Another story of Maine, that of the Great North Woods, is documented well by Louise Dickinson Rich, who for many years lived in the woods in the Rangeley area. I have used excerpts from both *We Took to the Woods* and *My Neck of the Woods* to portray her poignant and beautiful story.

Maine: A Portrait is a compilation of my views of Maine throughout the different seasons, both in photographs and in essay form. I have included visual stories of Maine's fishermen and loggers—the independent self-assured and taciturn Mainer exists indeed.

Fishing boats at Manset

The natural order in Maine is absolutely incredible to photograph. From the rocky coast, tidal pools, and sea smoke to the great rivers, the Great North Woods, and Mount Katahdin—no matter the season, its beauty remains constant yet always fresh.

Lobster buoys, Corea

Maine is a state with many moods and impressive visages. It is an enormous story of the natural order, which David Thoreau opened my eyes to so vividly in his book *The Maine Woods*. Native Americans had known it for so many centuries prior. Maine has many other stories, and I do not profess to tell them all. Rather, I attempt to provide a significant overview of this beautiful piece of geography and its people, in a given moment of time, from my vantage point. In addition, my walk in Mr. Porter's footsteps is presumptive on my part, and his lifetime's work I could not hope to emulate. *Maine, A Portrait* is instead a token of my respect for this great artist. He inspired me and showed me the way.

I wish to thank Connie and David John for their friendship and lore of Maine. They led me to Louise Dickinson Rich and the moose. I wish to thank Timothy Whelan for his sound advice and his inventory on books by Eliot Porter. I am grateful to the many individuals—the fishermen, the loggers—for their insights and their helping me to form this presentation. My wife Joan who shared the whole mile with me is always my soundest critic and helpmate, and without her support, these books would not have happened. Now that she has retired, we are together in these studies, which makes my travels so much better. Thanks to Neale Sweet and Michael Steere of Down East Books for seeing Maine as I have and for publishing my work. Thanks also to Black Sheep Creative for their sensitive design. The natural order makes Joan and I happy; we appreciate its beauty. I thank my maker for the opportunity to be an integral part of this story.

Introduction

Lobster boats at Bar Harbor

Maine is one of those rare places with the power to provide spectacular observations that leave its visitors with haunting images of beauty and the unique characteristics of its people. The urge to compose a book of these images is overpowering to me. The quality of light and colors and patterns of the seasons presents an array of visages that I feel compelled to record. Though I am "from away," I find myself very much at home with Maine's splendor and its people. My portrait of Maine is all about nature, as I find the natural order intrinsic to my way of seeing and expressing life.

I have chosen to organize this imagery into two regions—the coast and the Great North Woods. The story of Maine reveals a natural order. The state's present geography has evolved from the collision of two tectonic plates, which resulted in massive upheavals of an old sea and the formation of the Appalachian fold that extends from the eastern seaboard of Maine to Georgia. Great northern glaciers carved out immense valleys, and in their retreat redirected rivers to their present courses and a trail of age-old debris made up of rocks and stones. The melting ice age raised the level of the sea—as it continues to do to this day—creating grand estuaries of flooded river plains. The atmosphere and weather are tempered by cold arctic air masses that move south over land and meet up with the warm Gulf Stream air offshore in the North Atlantic Ocean. The result is a constant movement of moisture and temperature that creates uncertain and exciting weather conditions. The rotation of the earth in relation to the moon creates some of the most dramatic ocean tides in the world in Maine—some reach heights of thirty feet or more. All of these factors have created an environment that dominates all who live here. The land begrudgingly yielded a foothold to man, first along the eastern coast, known as "downeast," and then inland toward the Great North Woods. Molded by their efforts to live in this environment, Maine natives, first as Native Americans and eventually as western European settlers, have become reserved, independent, and laconic.

From the brilliant and chilly mornings in the mountains to the wild woods south of Fort Kent and from the beauty of fall at Mount Katahdin, Moosehead Lake, the Allagash River, and Baxter State Park to the lovely clear lakes and river corridors of the Rangeley and Sebago area, the environment of the Great North Woods controls the seasonal visitations of man. Somehow, a few hardy individuals stay to live through its long, snowy winters and the spring confrontations with black flies and mosquitoes. The coast, with its broad sand beaches in the southeast that gradually become more dramatic and rocky as one travels northeast, is more forgiving and a destination for many in any season. Most of the year, pleasure boats cruise, ferries run, and workboats tend their pots and nets guided by a string of remote lighthouses. From Lubec where the sun first rises on the U.S. mainland and Schoodic Point and Mount Desert Island with its Acadia National Park to the stunning harbors of Stonington, Boothbay, Bath, and Ogunquit with their colorful fishing villages to the myriad of tranquil-looking islands that dot the water in between, the coast beckons.

In the state of Maine, picture postcard scenes abound. It is a special land, where man is but one species in a magnificent display of nature. In this special place, nature molds the man as much as man molds the land. It is a way of life that all Mainers work hard to preserve.

Workboats at Boothbay Harbor

The Coast

House in Kennebunkport

From the broad sandy beaches of Kittery Point in the south to the quiet Popham Beach State Park near Bath, the gentle rise of the shore punctuated by rocky crags provides the summer beachgoer with ideal sunning after each long winter. Because of the flow of currents, the water remains cold year-round. The cold Labrador current hugs the Maine coast while, further offshore, the Gulf Stream pushing north to Nova Scotia traps this cold current, keeping it close to shore. Swimming is limited in these waters. Many small summer communities have grown up along the coast as Boston city workers looked beyond Cape Cod for a quiet place to relax. Over the years, these popular summer places have become year-round homes as workers retired to them. Towns such as York, Ogunquit, Perkins Cove, Wells, Kennebunkport, Biddeford Pool, and Old Orchard Beach have all developed into destination communities with boutiques, fine restaurants, bed and breakfasts, and beautiful old hotels while older towns such as the established Kennebunk, Biddeford, Saco, Scarborough, and Portland (Maine's largest city) have only gotten more interesting. Some became well-planned towns where gracious living relied on old money. Others went through the coastal industrial growth of the early 19th century and are now rebuilding infrastructure as well as their communities for a better quality of living.

From Kittery Point to Portland, the traffic is busy and commerce is strong. Inland, congestion drops off sharply, and small farms and rolling hills form the countryside. At Portland, offshore islands and lighthouses become profuse as one heads northeast. From Brunswick to Eastport, long landmass fingers of rock and earth created by the movement and friction of retreating glaciers following old riverbeds that led into the ocean form an irregular coastline.

Along the way, small fishing villages edge quiet protected harbors and even more islands can be spotted offshore. Some of these sites had been inhabited by Native Americans and were most likely visited by Europeans many centuries earlier.

During the early days of the colonies, exploration was by sea, and settlements depended on the sea for a livelihood. Abundant fish, lobster, and shellfish catches provided fishermen with an income and their neighbors and families with food. Early shipbuilding eventually developed into a Maine craft of world renown, and the state's shipyards built great seaworthy vessels of superior sailing ability.

Today, efforts continue to keep the wooden boatbuilding craft alive. All along the coast, one can find small boatbuilders producing some of the most seaworthy craft available. A school for wooden boat building in Brooklin provides classes each summer that cover several aspects of small boat building for over 750 students from all over the world. The fishing and lobster industries, however, are diminishing as the ocean stocks become depleted by overfishing and the increased costs of fishing (insurance and boat maintenance) are compounded by reduced profits due to catch limits. As a result, it is difficult to make a livelihood fishing today, and many fishermen have quit. Consequently, some of the old and colorful fishing villages are slowly converting to ports for pleasure sailboats and cruising boats for nature watching or island visiting. In the not too distant future, Baileys Island, Port Clyde, Belfast, Stonington, Bass Harbor, Jonesport, Lubec, and Eastport will follow the lead of Kennebunkport, Boothbay, Camden, Rockport, Northeast Harbor, Winter Harbor, and Bar Harbor to become fashionable summer oases for the yachtsmen and their families, requiring supporting fashionable infrastructure. The models are Kennebunkport, Boothbay, and Bar Harbor, which are stylish and upscale and feature summer festivals that bring a rush of commerce. During June, July, and August, tourism is the driving economic force in these communities. I prefer to visit these communities in May or late September when the crowds are more manageable. From Ellsworth and Bar Harbor to Eastport the economic development to tourism will be considerably slower, which continues to allow a slower paced traveler to poke and probe along the coast with exceptional results.

A canoe under construction at the Wooden Boat School in Brooklin

Facing page: The road to Monhegan Island Lighthouse

Above: A derelict vessel in Rockport

Right: A view across Rockport Harbor

Facing page: Summer at Little Pond

The Coast

Tidal stream in South Addison

Facing page: Birches and grass near Sieur de Monts Spring, Acadia National Park

from Rachel Carson's The Edge of the Sea

Preface

Like the sea itself, the shore fascinates us who return to it, the place of our dim ancestral beginnings. In the recurrent rhythms of tides and surf and in the varied life of the tide lines there is the obvious attraction of movement and change and beauty. There is also, I am convinced, a deeper fascination born of inner meaning and significance.

When we go down to the low-tide line, we enter a world that is as old as the earth itself—the primeval meeting place of the elements of earth and water, a place of compromise and conflict and eternal change. For us as living creatures it has special meaning as an area in or near which some entity that could be distinguished as Life first drifted in shallow waters—reproducing, evolving, yielding that endlessly varied stream of living things that has surged through time and space to occupy the earth.

To understand the shore, it is not enough to catalog its life. Understanding comes only when, standing on a beach, we can sense the long rhythms of earth and sea that sculptured its land forms and produced the rock and sand of which it is composed; when we can sense with the eye and ear of the mind the surge of life beating always at its shores—blindly, inexorably pressing for a foothold. To understand the life of the shore, it is not enough to pick up an empty shell and say "This is a murex," or "That is an angel wing." True understanding demands intuitive comprehension of the whole life of the creature that once inhabited this empty shell: how it survived amid surf and storms,

Tidal pool at Grindstone Point

Facing page: The shoreline at Swans Island

what were its enemies, how it found food and reproduced its kind, what were its relations to the particular sea world in which it lived.

The seashores of the world may be divided into three basic types: the rugged shores of rock, the sand beaches, and the coral reefs. . . . Each has its typical community of plants and animals.

The Marginal World

The edge of the sea is a strange and beautiful place. All through the long history of Earth it has been an area of unrest where waves have broken heavily against the land, where the tides have pressed forward over the continents, receded, and then returned. For no two successive days is the shore line precisely the same. Not only do the tides advance and retreat in their eternal rhythms, but the level of the sea itself is never at rest. It rises or falls as the glaciers melt or grow, as the floor of the deep ocean basins shifts under its increasing load of sediments, or as the earth's crust along the continental margins warps up or down in adjustment to strain and tension. Today a little more land may belong to the sea, tomorrow a little less. Always the edge of the sea remains an elusive and indefinable boundary.

The shore has a dual nature, changing with the swing of the tides, belonging now to the land, now to the sea. On the ebb tide it knows the harsh extremes of the land world, being exposed to heat and cold, to wind, to rain and drying sun. On the flood tide it is a water world, returning briefly to the relative stability of the open sea.

Only the most hardy and adaptable can survive in a region so mutable, yet the area between the tide lines is crowded with plants and animals. In this difficult world of the shore, life displays its enormous toughness and vitality by occupying almost every conceivable niche. Visibly, it carpets the intertidal rocks; or half hidden, it descends into fissures and crevices, or hides under boulders, or lurks in the wet gloom of sea caves. Invisibly, where the casual observer would say there is no life, it lies deep in the sand, in burrows and tubes and passageways. It tunnels into solid

Seaweed at Owls Head

rock and bores into peat and clay. It encrusts weeds or drifting spars or the hard chitinous shell of a lobster. It exists minutely, as the film of bacteria that spreads over a rock surface or a wharf piling; as spheres of protozoa, small as pinpricks, sparking at the surface of the sea; and as Lilliputian beings swimming through dark pools that lie between the grains of sand.

The shore is an ancient world, for as long as there has been an earth and sea there has been this place of the meeting of land and water. Yet it is a world that keeps alive the sense of continuing creation and of the relentless drive of life. Each time that I enter it, I gain some new awareness of its beauty and its deeper meanings, sensing that intricate fabric of life by which one creature is linked with another, and each with its surroundings.

Crashing waves at Schoodic Point

In my thoughts of the shore, one place stands apart for its revelation of exquisite beauty. It is a pool hidden within a cave that one can visit only rarely and briefly when the lowest of the year's low tides fall below it, and perhaps from that very fact it acquires some of its special beauty. Choosing such a tide, I hoped for a glimpse of the pool. The ebb was to fall early in the morning. I knew that if the wind held from the northwest and no interfering swell ran in from a distant storm the level of the sea should drop below the entrance to the pool. There had been sudden ominous showers in the night, with rain like handfuls of gravel flung on the roof. When I looked out into the early morning the sky was full of a gray dawn light but the sun had not yet risen. Water and air were pallid. Across the bay the moon was a luminous disc in the western sky, suspended above the dim line of distant shore—the full August moon, drawing the tide to the low, low levels of the threshold of the alien sea world. As I watched, a gull flew by, above the spruces. Its breast was rosy with the light of the unrisen sun. The day was, after all, to be fair.

Later, as I stood above the tide near the entrance to the pool, the promise of that rosy light was sustained. From the base of the steep wall of rock on which I stood, a moss-covered ledge jutted seaward into deep water. In the surge at the rim of the ledge the dark fronds of oarweeds swayed, smooth and gleaming as leather. The projecting ledge was the path to the small hidden cave and its pool. Occasionally a swell, stronger than the rest, rolled smoothly over the rim and broke in foam against the cliff. But the intervals between such swells were long enough to admit me to the ledge and long enough for a glimpse of that fairy pool, so seldom and so briefly exposed.

And so I knelt on the wet carpet of sea moss and looked back into the dark cavern that held the pool in a shallow basin. The floor of the cave was only a few inches below the roof, and a mirror had been created in which all that grew on the ceiling was reflected in the still water below.

Under water that was clear as glass the pool was carpeted with green sponge. Gray patches of sea squirts glistened on the ceiling and colonies of soft coral were a pale apricot color. In the moment when I looked into the cave a little elfin starfish hung down, suspended by the merest thread, perhaps by only a single tube foot. It reached down to touch its own reflection, so perfectly delineated that there might have been, not one starfish, but two. The beauty of the reflected images and of the limpid pool itself was the poignant beauty of things that are ephemeral, existing only until the sea should return to fill the little cave.

Whenever I go down into this magical zone of the low water of the spring tides, I look for the most delicately beautiful of all the shore inhabitants—flowers that are not plant but animal, blooming on the threshold of the deeper sea. In that fairy cave I was not disappointed. Hanging from its roof were the pendent flowers of the hydroid Tubularia, pale pink, fringed and delicate as the wind flower. Here were creatures so exquisitely fashioned that they seemed unreal, their beauty too fragile to exist in a world of crushing force. Yet every detail was functionally useful, every stalk and hydranth and petal-like tentacle fashioned for dealing with the realities of existence. I knew that they were merely waiting, in that moment of the tide's ebbing, for the return of the sea. Then in the rush of the water, in the surge of surf and the pressure of the incoming tide, the delicate flower heads would stir with life. They would sway on their slender stalks, and their long tentacles would sweep the returning water, finding in it all that they needed for life.

And so in that enchanted place on the threshold of the sea

Starfish at low tide, Grindstone Point

the realities that possessed my mind were far from those of the land world I had left an hour before. . . .

There is a common thread that links these scenes—the spectacle of life in all its varied manifestations as it has appeared, evolved, and sometimes died out. Underlying the beauty of the spectacle there is meaning and significance. It is the elusiveness of that meaning that haunts us, that sends us again and again into the natural world where the key to the riddle is hidden. It sends us back to the edge of the sea, where the drama of life played its first scene on earth and perhaps even its prelude; where the forces of evolution are at work today, as they have been since the appearance of what we know as life; and where the spectacle of living creatures faced by the cosmic realities of their world is crystal clear.

The seawall at Acadia National Park

The Rocky Shores

Tortured rock at Port Clyde

When the tide is high on a rocky shore, when its brimming fullness creeps up almost to the bayberry and the junipers where they come down from the land, one might easily suppose that nothing at all lived in or on or under these waters of the sea's edge. For nothing is visible. Nothing except here and there a little group of herring gulls, for at high tide the gulls rest on ledges of rock, dry above the surf and the spray, and they tuck their yellow bills under their feathers and doze away the hours of the rising water. Then all the creatures of the tidal rocks are hidden from view, but the gulls know what is there, and they know that in time the water will fall away again and give them entrance to the strip between the tide lines.

When the tide is rising the shore is a place of unrest, with the surge leaping high over jutting rocks and running in lacy cascades of foam over the landward side of massive boulders. But on the ebb it is more peaceful, for then the waves do not have behind them the push of the inward pressing tides. There is no particular drama about the turn of the tide, but presently a zone of wetness shows on the gray rock slopes, and offshore the incoming swells begin to swirl and break over hidden ledges. Soon the rocks that the high tide had concealed rise into view and glisten with the wetness left on them by the receding water.

Small, dingy snails move about over rocks that are slippery with the growth of infinitesimal green plants; the snails scraping, scraping, to find food before the surf returns.

Like drifts of old snow no longer white, the barnacles come into view; they blanket rocks and old spars wedged into rock

Herring gull at Schoodic Point

crevices, and their sharp cones are sprinkled over empty mussel shells and lobster-pot buoys and the hard stipes of deep-water seaweeds, all mingled in the flotsam of the tide.

Meadows of brown rockweeds appear on the gently sloping rocks of the shore as the tide imperceptibly ebbs. Smaller patches of green weed, stringy as mermaids' hair, begin to turn white and crinkly where the sun has dried them.

Now the gulls, that lately rested on the higher ledges, pace with grave intentness along the walls of rock, and they probe under the hanging curtains of weed to find crabs and sea urchins.

In the low places little pools and gutters are left where the water trickles and gurgles and cascades in miniature waterfalls, and many of the dark caverns between and under the rocks are floored with still mirrors holding the reflections of delicate creatures that shun the light and avoid the shock of waves—the cream-colored flowers of the small anemones and the pink fingers of soft coral, pendent from the rocky ceiling.

In the calm world of the deeper rock pools, now undisturbed by the tumult of incoming waves, crabs sidle along the walls, their claws busily touching, feeling, exploring for bits of food. The pools are gardens of color composed of the delicate green and ocher-yellow of encrusting sponge, the pale pink of hydroids that stand like clusters of fragile spring flowers, the bronze and electric-blue gleams of the Irish moss, the old-rose beauty of the coralline algae.

And over it all there is the smell of low tide, compounded of the faint, pervasive smell of worms and snails and jellyfish and crabs—the sulphur smell of sponge, the iodine smell of rockweed, and the salt smell of the rime that glitters on the sun-dried rocks.

One of my own favorite approaches to a rocky seacoast is by a rough path through an evergreen forest that has its own peculiar enchantment. It is usually an early morning tide that takes me along that forest path, so that the light is still pale and fog drifts in from the sea beyond. It is almost a ghost forest, for among the living spruce and balsam are many dead trees—some still erect, some sagging earthward, some lying on the floor of the forest. All the trees, the living and the dead, are clothed with green and silver crusts of lichens. Tufts of the bearded lichen or old man's beard hang from the branches like bits of sea mist tangled there. Green woodland mosses and a yielding carpet of reindeer moss cover the ground. In the quiet of that place even the voice of the surf is reduced to a whispered echo and the sounds of the forest

Old and new growth at Acadia National Park

are but the ghosts of sound—the faint sighings of evergreen needles in the moving air; the creaks and heavier groans of half-fallen trees resting against their neighbors and rubbing bark against bark; the light rattling fall of a dead branch broken under the feet of a squirrel and sent bouncing and ricocheting earthward.

But finally the path emerges from the dimness of the deeper forest and comes to a place where the sound of surf rises above the forest sounds—the hollow boom of the sea, rhythmic and insistent, striking against the rocks, falling away, rising again.

Up and down the coast the line of the forest is drawn sharp and clean on the edge of a seascape of surf and sky and rocks. The softness of sea fog blurs the contours of the rocks; gray water and gray mists merge offshore in a dim and vaporous world that might be a world of creation, stirring with new life.

The sense of newness is more than illusion born of the early morning light and the fog, for this is in very fact a young coast. It was only yesterday in the life of the earth that the sea came in as the coast subsided, filling the valleys and rising about the slopes of the hills, creating these rugged shores where rocks rise out of the sea and evergreen forests come down to the coastal rocks. Once this shore was like the ancient land to the south, where the nature of the coast has changed little during the millions of years since the sea and the wind and the rain created its sands and shaped them into dune and beach and offshore bar and shoal. The northern coast, too, had its flat coastal plain bordered by wide beaches of sand. Behind these lay a landscape of rocky hills alternating with valleys that had been worn by streams and deepened and sculptured by glaciers. The hills were formed of gneiss and other crystalline rocks resistant to erosion; the

A tree twisted by the elements at Schoodic Point

The Edge of the Sea

lowlands had been created in beds of weaker rocks like sandstones, shale, and marl.

Then the scene changed. From a point somewhere in the vicinity of Long Island the flexible crust of the earth tilted downward under the burden of a vast glacier. The regions we know as eastern Maine and Nova Scotia were pressed down into the earth, some areas being carried as much as 1,200 feet beneath the sea. All of the northern coastal plain was drowned. Some of its more elevated parts are now offshore shoals, the fishing banks off the New England and Canadian coasts—Georges, Browns, Quereau, the Grand Bank. None of it remains above the sea except here and there a high and isolated hill, like the present island of Monhegan, which in ancient times must have stood above the coastal plain as a bold monadnock.

Where the mountainous ridges and the valleys lay at an angle to the coast, the sea ran far up between the hills and occupied the valleys. This was the origin of the deeply indented and exceedingly irregular coast that is characteristic of much of Maine. The long narrow estuaries of the Kennebec, the Sheepscot, the Damariscotta and many other rivers run inland a score of miles. These salt-water rivers, now arms of the sea, are the drowned valleys in which grass and trees grew in a geologic yesterday. The rocky, forested ridges between them probably looked much as they do today. Off shore, chains of islands jut out obliquely into the sea, one beyond another—half-submerged ridges of the former land mass. . . .

For the most part, the ruggedness of this coast is the ruggedness of the hills themselves. There are none of the wave-cut stacks and arches that distinguish older coasts or coasts of softer rocks. In a few, exceptional places the work of the waves may be seen. The south shore of Mount Desert Island is exposed to heavy pounding by surf; there the waves have cut out Anemone Cave and are working at Thunder Hole to batter through the roof of the small cave into which the surf roars at high tide.

In places the sea washes the foot of a steep cliff produced by the shearing effect of earth pressure along fault lines. Cliffs on Mount Desert—Schooner Head, Great Head, and Otter—tower a hundred feet or more above the sea. Such imposing structures might be taken for wave-cut cliffs if one did not know the geologic history of the region.

Here and there on the predominantly rocky coast of northern New England there are small beaches of sand, pebbles, or cobblestones. These have a varied origin. Some came from glacial debris that covered the rocky surface when the land tilted and the sea came in. Boulders and pebbles often are carried in from deeper water offshore by seaweeds that have gripped them firmly with their "holdfasts." Storm waves then dislodge weed and stone and cast them on the shore. Even without the aid of weeds, waves carry in a considerable volume of sand, gravel, shell fragments, and even boulders. These occasional sandy or pebbly

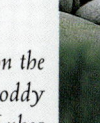

Smooth rocks on the shore at West Quoddy Head Lighthouse, Lubec

Facing page: Otter Cliffs of Acadia National Park

beaches are almost always in protected, incurring shores or dead-end coves, where the waves can deposit debris but from which they cannot easily remove it.

When, on those coastal rocks between the serrate line of spruces and the surf, the morning mists conceal the lighthouses and fishing boats and all other reminders of man, they also blur the sense of time and one might easily imagine that the sea came in only yesterday to create this particular line of coast. Yet the creatures that inhabit the intertidal rocks have had time to establish themselves here, replacing the fauna of the beaches of sand and mud that probably bordered the older coast. Out of the same sea that rose over the northern coast of New England, drowning the coastal plain and coming to rest against the hard uplands, the larvae of the rock dwellers came—the blindly searching larvae that drift in the ocean currents ready to colonize whatever suitable land may lie in their path or to die, if no such landfall is their lot.

The Enduring Sea

Now I hear the sea sounds about me; the night high tide is rising, swirling with a confused rush of waters against the rocks below my study window. Fog has come into the bay from the open sea, and it lies over water and over the land's edge, seeping back into the spruces and stealing softly among the juniper and the bayberry. The restive waters, the cold wet breath of the fog, are of a world in which man is an uneasy trespasser; he punctuates the night with the complaining groan and grunt of a foghorn, sensing the power and menace of the sea.

Bass Harbor Head Lighthouse   Facing page: Sea smoke and lobster boats, Stonington

Maine: A Portrait

Calais, Lubec, Cutler, Machias, Roque Bluffs State Park, and Jonesport

This is an area of Maine where among the blueberry fields stretching over barrens, little coves and their fishing villages present a more peaceful "downeast" adventure than further south. This part of the coast also offers some of the world's largest tides and earliest sunrises in the U.S. Calais is an entry point to and from Canada, and nearby Moosehorn National Wildlife Refuge gives one a sense of the pure Maine. Southeast in Lubec, one can cross the international bridge and enter New Brunswick, Canada. Here is Campobello Island, summer home of Franklin Delano Roosevelt. Southeast of Lubec one will find West Quoddy Head and its West Quoddy Head Lighthouse and Quoddy Head State Park, which marks the beginning of the stunning Gold Coast that ends at the harbor in Cutler a bit further south. Just beyond Cutler lies Machias, Roque Bluffs State Park, with its little gem of a rocky beach, and Jonesport. From Cutler or Jonesport, tour boats are available to take visitors to Machias Seal Island, New Brunswick, where from blinds one can view nesting Arctic and common terns, common Murres, razor-billed auks, and Atlantic puffins.

Schoodic Point

One of my very favorite locations on the Maine coast is a part of Acadia National Park that sees far fewer visitors. Schoodic Point is a stunning peninsula with a pink granite promontory that drops into the Atlantic at its easternmost point. Its solitude

Facing page: Atlantic puffin

This home at Wonsqueak Harbor was once used for a fishnet manufacturing operation

beckons. Coming off the drive around Schoodic Point, visitors should stop at Wonsqueak Harbor for a picturesque view of a former fishnet-making building across the harbor. It is now a home, with a red canoe that provides a colorful prop at both high and low tides. Nearby Winter Harbor with its many stately summer homes is where I found Grindstone Point, which has the finest tidal pools that I have seen in Maine. At low tide, you can find red starfish. On the way to Corea, a traditional and colorful fishing village that enjoys a small, safe harbor, is Prospect Harbor with its fish processing plant.

The Coast

Left: Jonesport Harbor at low tide

Below left: Dinghy by a tidal stream, Pembroke

Below right: Derelict lobster boat, Jonesport

Maine: A Portrait

View of Lubec

The Coast

Southwest Harbor

Up for the winter, Bass Harbor

Mount Desert Island and Acadia National Park

Many park enthusiasts claim that Acadia National Park is their favorite in the U.S. Seeded by the generosity of John D. Rockefeller, it is a major portion of Mount Desert Island. Approached from Ellsworth, the island's main town is the trendy and popular Bar Harbor. In the center of the island is the park itself, which reaches eastward to the Atlantic Ocean. South lies exclusive Northeast Harbor, quaint Somesville, with the only fiord on the East Coast, traditional Southwest Harbor, and colorful Bass Harbor, with its popular lighthouse anchored on the rocky shore. Other small villages intersperse ocean landscapes, tidal marshlands, and mountain terrain. At the heart of Acadia National Park is Cadillac Mountain, rising 1,530 feet from the Atlantic, which allows a magnificent 360-degree view of sea and island. Reached by car, the drive is part of the Park Loop Road, a circular drive that winds around the island, passing the ocean (Thunder Hole, Otter Point, and Sand Beach) at times while traversing the mountains at others. Its seascape vistas are unparalleled. Camping is popular and the two park campgrounds are quite different and beautiful. The popular Blackwoods campground is located near Bar Harbor in dense woods with a short walk to the rocky cliffs. More remote, private, and less congested is the Seawall Campground, also located in fir forests. Nearby is a lovely rocky shore with great tide pools and quiet sunsets. Also close by are the Wonderland Trail and the Ships Cove Trail that lead one to a sea of surpassing beauty. We like Seawall because we can eat lobster right on the pier while watching the fishing boats conduct their daily work. In nearby Manset one can watch an exclusive boatbuilder creating elegant sailing yachts. Many offshore destinations can be reached via ferries or private cruise boats from Bar Harbor (to Nova Scotia), Northeast Harbor (to Cranberry Islands), and Bass Harbor (to Swans Island and Long Island).

Bass Harbor Head Lighthouse

Ash berries and spruce cones at Acadia National Park

Deer Isle, Stonington, Castine, and Blue Hill

Stonington is quintessential "downeast." Its long-established fishing community surrounds the rock harbor and looks out on many offshore islands. It is breathtakingly beautiful. This is where Eliot Porter photographed for his Maine book. This is

Above: The Bar Harbor Inn

Left: This nontraditional Maine home in Castine was converted from a barn

Right: The schooner Margaret Todd sails out of Bar Harbor

The Coast

Maine Maritime Academy training boat, Castine

The Abbott School, Castine   Facing page: Winter shore at Deer Isle

Maine: A Portrait

Golden chain tree, Seal Harbor

Lupines and beach roses at Seal Cove

Facing page: Antique lobster traps at Bass Harbor

Maine: A Portrait

Stonington

Granite and mooring chain, Stonington

Lobster boat, Bernard

New traps and buoys, Stonington

Lobsterman's tool kit

The Coast

Dusk at Stonington Harbor

Facing page: Pumpkin Island Lighthouse and sea smoke across Eggemoggin Reach

The Coast

where artists paint and photographers shoot to capture Maine at its traditional best. Its granite quarries conjure up images of labor gangs struggling with the core of the earth, while lobster pounds and colorful boats with their captain and crew reveal the same manual work, which is slowly dying out as stocks become depleted. From here, boats take visitors to Isle au Haut and Vinalhaven. Nearby Eggemoggin Reach Lighthouse is a gem that displays different faces with different tides. Blue Hill is the home to artists, musicians, and writers, probably the most well-known of which is E.B. White who wrote *Charlotte's Web*. Near here, in Brooklin, is the famous Wooden Boat School, which keeps alive the traditional craftsmanship of an earlier time, and south on the peninsula is Castine, a picturesque village with many classic older homes that border the historic campus of the Maine Maritime Academy. Heading south from Ellsworth on Coastal Route 1, you'll drive through several seafaring towns, including Searsport, Belfast, Northport, and Lincolnville. Each are worthy of a stop and offer beauty, tradition, delightful architecture, a maritime museum and terrific bookstore (Searsport), antique shops, and art galleries.

View from Vinalhaven

This small boat was built at the Wooden Boat School in Brooklin

Camden, Rockport, and Rockland

This heartland of Maine arts calls to mind the names of Andrew and Jamie Wyeth and the Olson House, The Farnsworth Art Museum, Rockport's Center for Maine Contemporary Art, the Camden Opera House, and the Maine Photographic

Low tide at Glen Cove

The Olson House in Cushing was made famous by painter Andrew Wyeth

Buoys on Vinalhaven

Camden Harbor

Workshops; all are anchored by the tony community of Camden, which is filled with some of Maine's finest bed-and-breakfasts, quaint shops, boutiques, good bookstores, and a busy little harbor. From the top of Mount Battie, reached by car or foot trails, one can see miles of coast on a clear day. Right next door to Camden, Rockport is a pleasing community with a narrow harbor and a marble statue of André, the seal. A short drive south brings one to Rockland, an industrial town that is growing up. The Farnsworth Art Museum and the Wyeth Center are located here, along with several galleries, interesting shops, and good architecture. Rockland is also a departure point for the Vinalhaven, Northhaven, and Matinicus Island ferries, and boasts two unique lighthouses guarding its large harbor. Further south, Port Clyde also has a lighthouse as well as a lovely harbor and a ferry to Monhegan Island. Head back up to Thomaston, and drive south along the River Road and one will arrive in Cushing. The Olson House, which was the subject for Andrew Wyeth's famous "Christina's World," is found there.

Boothbay Harbor

Boothbay has a special ambiance. For three months it is the classic sea resort town and for six months it shuts down tight. From its Ocean Point Drive to Newagen, one is never far from dramatic and beautiful seascapes. The harbor is bounded by hotels, restaurants, and boutiques, and is interspersed with working boats and lobster pounds. Summer homes

Nat Wilson's sailmaking shop in East Boothbay

The Coast

Storm clouds over Cushing

The Bay Lady sailing in Boothbay Harbor

Shed and dinghy in East Boothbay

Ocean view from East Boothbay

The Coast

of the rich and famous abound and the more ordinary summer visitor crowds the area to appreciate the color and beauty. Cruises take visitors whale, seal, and puffin watching or to visit the beautiful and striking Monhegan Island, where many artists paint. Boothbay is filled to capacity for the Windjammer Days Festival in July which signals the start of the summer season with tall ships and a display of fireworks over the harbor. If you want to try something special, visit the Fisherman's Wharf Restaurant for a locally caught Maine lobster and watch the sun go down over the harbor while eating blueberry pie on the deck. You may well think you are in heaven.

Pemaquid Point, Damariscotta, and Monhegan Island

On the way to Pemaquid Point and its memorable lighthouse is New Harbor, where one can also take a sightseeing boat to Monhegan Island. During peak season, one must make reservations in advance for a seat on the boat and a room on the island, but it is well worth it. This is one of Maine's most picturesque locations. One third of the island is a small village inhabited mostly by fishermen and artists. The rest of the island is forest and rocky coast and can be reached by paths wandering through and along both. Nowhere is one more than a twenty-minute hike to the center, yet the variations of environment will surprise you. It is a special island, as is Pemaquid Point on the mainland with Pemaquid Lighthouse and the Fisherman's Museum and just slightly north, Fort William Henry. The town of Damariscotta, built along the Damariscotta River, was a clipper-shipbuilding town during the 1800s, and its homes, some with widow's walks, reflect this heritage. On the outskirts of town one will discover the charming Round Top Center for the Arts.

Facing page: Windjammer Days festival at Boothbay Harbor   *Pemaquid Point Lighthouse*

The Coast

Marshall Point Light at Port Clyde

Facing page: Monhegan Island Inn with Manana Island in the background

Seaspray at Pemaquid Point

Workboat with net, Southport

Facing page: Friendship Harbor

The German Lutheran Church and cemetery in Waldoboro

The Coast

New Harbor lobster boat Bonnie Jean II

Bailey Island lobster boat

Popham Beach State Park

Guided-missile cruisers like these are built for the Navy at Bath Iron Works

Wiscasset, Bath, Popham Beach, Brunswick, Orrs Island, and Bailey Island

Wiscasset, which is nestled along the Sheepscot River, has many lovely captains' homes telling a story of its past as a maritime community. South of Wiscasset one finds Bath, a current shipbuilding center and home to the Maine Maritime Museum. From the bridge over the Kennebec River, one can see Bath Iron Works and the destroyers it builds for the Navy. Detour southeast and one will arrive at Popham Beach State Park, a sunbather's dream for its wide, shallow, soft sand beaches. Brunswick offers great architecture, Bowdoin College, home to many of Maine's finest writers and thinkers, and a fine art museum. East of Brunswick, at the end of Route 24, Orrs Island and Bailey Island and their fishing villages are well worth exploring for their charm and beauty.

Lobster crossing, Bailey Island

Dinghy with traps and buoys at Bailey Island

Traditional clapboard-sided house in Harpswell

Facing page: Hendricks Head Lighthouse, Southport

View of Southport Harbor

The Coast

Bailey Island lobster shack

Home on Monhegan Island

Kennebunkport church

Facing page: Portland Head Lighthouse   Cape Neddick Lighthouse, York

The Coast

Dories all in a row: low tide at Salsbury Cove

A single sea-polished cobble on Grindstone Point

A frigid morning at Stonington Harbor

Lobster shack, Bernard Harbor

Swans Island ferry

The Coast

Path to Long Pond, Chain of Ponds north of Stratton

Facing page: Mother moose and calf near Wilsons Mills

The Great North Woods

Sometimes called the "Great North Woods" or the "Great North Country" or the "North Country" or simply the "Country" or the "Woods," the Maine woods is home to many creatures, including moose, deer, eagle, loon, and bear. In the south, the woods begin at Sebago Lake and move northeast through Lewiston, Augusta, Waterville, Newport, and continue north. To the west they cross the New Hampshire border. They reach north through Rangeley and spread east through Moosehead Lake and Baxter State Park, which is home to Mount Katahdin and the upper extremity of the Appalachian Trail. The woods rise up the Allagash and St. John Rivers to the Canadian border of New Brunswick, finding their limitation at Fort Kent and Madawaska. It is an immense area of dark woods broken up by crystal blue lakes, sparkling river corridors, and a few roads in the east, which are interrupted by the towns of Houlton, Presque Isle, and Caribou. At different points moving further inland and to the north, paved roads tend to stop and logging roads take over. This is wild country where mosquitoes and black flies reign in the spring, and snow and cold last seven months of the year. It is stunning here when the poignant cry of the loon echoes over the lakes and the bellow of moose fills the shallow valleys. It can make man feel extremely alone. In the Maine woods, man is only a guest. The forests are dark and thick. "Blowdowns" prevent man from traveling through fallen timber easily and can confuse one's direction for even the most capable of woodsmen. In many areas, roads are limited solely to logging company trucks. These are rough, gated dirt roads with no trace of man for miles on end. The "sportsman" fishes and hunts under the watchful eye of a Maine guide. Cross-country skiing, snowshoeing, ice fishing, snowmobiling, and hunting are more than just pastimes, they provide a way for year-round living in the Great North Woods.

from Louise Dickinson Rich's
My Neck of the Woods
and We Took to the Woods

The North Country from My Neck of the Woods

Speaking relatively, I live in the far north—in the top, lefthand corner of Maine, just below the Canadian border—and there seems to be something about that country that fascinates people, even people who have never been there and never intend to go. Perhaps it's an inheritance passed down through the centuries from the time when for those who ventured away from the known coasts, the familiar landmarks, there was only one fixed point to steer by, the Pole Star, only one sure thing to guide them, the trembling needle pointing North. Or perhaps the North represents an idea, a state of mind, cold, detached, lonely and austere, sanctuary from the heat and confusion and indulgence of the modern world. Or perhaps again—and this is by far the most probable explanation—I'm making much ado about nothing, and the thing that interests chance acquaintances and sets them to asking questions about the North when they find out where I live, is nothing more or less than pure astonishment that anyone could be so misguided. Then there is a natural curiosity about such a life. So I try to tell them what the North is like.

In the first place, it is very, very beautiful. It's a country of lakes and forested mountains and tumbling rivers. It's beautiful all of the time. In the spring the new leaves of the birches and the blossoms of the maples look like wisps of green and red smoke blowing across the staid dark background of the fir and spruce, and the forest floor is carpeted with flowers—huge purple violets and tiny white ones, and the fragile wood sorrel, and the pink twin-sisters. The leafless rhodora blazes in the swamps. Then the thrushes sing high on the ridges in the arrowy light from the setting sun, and the red deer come down the slopes, stepping daintily into the

Facing page: Winter at Rangeley Lake

Late November goldenrod near Wilsons Mills

dusk of the valleys to drink. In the little villages and cross-roads around the lofty plateau of the lakes, the ancient lilacs break into a frenzy of bloom like lavender surf over the low houses, against which they lean. Even when it rains—and it rains quite a lot in Maine in the spring—it's beautiful. The curtains of the clouds hide the mountains, and all the world is gray and dim and full of the sound of water, and of the high sweet voices of the peepers in the bogs.

Summer is lovely, too, rich and full-blown. Cool, crisp nights follow blue sun-drenched days. Thunderstorms rattle around the mountains, rolling up one valley and down the next. The wild blueberries and raspberries ripen in hot clearings back in the woods, and the bear and foxes eat their fill. Everything smells wonderful—the pine, aromatic under the sun, the breeze blowing across a rock-ribbed pasture of cut hay, the very earth itself.

You have to see autumn in the North to believe it. The lakes are incredibly blue and the hillsides shout with color—orange and scarlet, yellow, and a crimson that is almost purple. In the night, the wild geese honk overhead beneath a full, burnished moon, fleeing south over the silvered ridges, from the smell of winter. The Borealis crackles up from the northern horizon, sending unearthly streamers of light a thousand miles long to waver and fade at the zenith. At sunrise the ground is white with hoar-frost, against which the tracks of the rabbits and deer and bob-cats are black and precise, and the water in the ruts of the woods road is skimmed lightly with ice. The air is like wine, thin and dry and chilled; and like wine, it exhilarates body and mind, so that the performance of great tasks and the dreaming of great dreams are as easy as turning over your hand.

And winter—what can I say about winter, when the wind,

Moxie Falls, West Forks

Icicles on cabin roof in Oquossoc

clean and knife-edged, pours down from the northwest, and the country is held in the grip of an iron cold. The snow falls and falls, steadily and soundlessly; or it drives down the bitter wind, scourging the land. The houses in the villages huddle together like sheep under its lash. The ice on the lakes silently thickens—one foot, eighteen inches, three feet—until it is as solid as living ledge under the heaviest load. In the dead silence of a windless night, it surrenders to the strain of its own increasing pressure, and as the rift runs across a lake—two, four, ten miles—a great half-human howl echoes through the mountains and up to the stars. It's a blood-chilling sound to hear, wild, lost, and despairing.

It doesn't snow all the time. Between storms the sky is deep sapphire, and all the shadows on the glittering white earth are violet. Nothing is familiar. The drifted snow lends grace and softness even to the stark architecture of a woodshed. In the villages and cross-roads, the windows of the besieged houses peer over eight-foot walls of snow at cars passing on the cleared roads, and every chimney wears constantly a plume of blue wood-smoke. Men shoveling paths and mittened women hanging out their stiffly frozen sheets call back and forth, and their voices are clear and bell-like in the crystal air. But winter is more than a time of ice and snow and cold. It's a time when more than the land is drained of life and emotion. It's a time for sitting and thinking, for being quiet, as the trees and rivers and lakes are quiet. That's what the North is like. Nobody lives there.

"Well, it's always interesting to hear another point of view outlined," as my sister says when she thoroughly disagrees with someone, but doesn't feel up to a fight. I suppose from one viewpoint, five and a half persons per square mile, which is about what we average, does add up to nobody. As for me, I consider that an ideal population, thick enough to be comforting, yet not so thick as to be cramping. Some of the five and a half have lived here all of their lives. Some were born here, moved elsewhere for a while, and then came back, and some came from away originally to settle here; but they all have a quality in common. I'm not sure whether it's a cause or an effect. To put it in the simple and unflattering words of a friend, Mabel Sias, "Do you people get the way you are, from living here, or were you all peculiar to start with? Why you all even look alike."

We really don't, of course, but I can see what she means. There is a prevalence of the long Yankee face, with its lean jaw, uncompromising mouth, observant eyes, but the universal resemblance is more than that. It lies in the expression on the faces, which do not give themselves over easily to the polite smile or the grimace of facile grief. It lies in the handling of the body—in the deceptively leisurely stride and the economy of gesture, in the almost animal-like ability to relax and to spring from relaxation into action. It lies, too, in the speech, which is laconic, and in the manner of speaking, which is deliberate and usually unimpassioned, and I'm afraid, frequently unintelligible to the Outsider. But these are only the visible clues to some fundamental common denominator.

What that denominator is, I find it hard to say; and anyhow, I'm tired of talking about my friends and acquaintances in terms of population averages and generic types, because they're a large part of the reason why I like the North. The landscape is very beautiful, as I have said, but it's the figures in the landscape that make it interesting. To me they are different from people anywhere else I have been, and they make more sense in the things they do and say.

We Took to the Woods – Chapter 1

There is nothing park-like about this northwestern-most corner of Maine. Here, between two ranges of mountains, the Boundry Mountains and the Blue Mountains, lies a high, wild valley, the basin that holds the Rangeley Lakes. The country is criss-crossed with ridges, dotted with swamps and logans, and covered with dense forest. There are very few people living here,

Antique truck and wooden snowplow, Oquossoc

and no roads down into what we call The Outside. There are a few narrow trails, but travel through the woods is so difficult, with the swamps, blowdowns and underbrush, that the lakes have remained what they were to the Indians, the main thoroughfare.

I like to think of the lakes coming down from the north of us like a giant staircase to the sea. Kennebago to Rangeley to Cupsuptic, down they drop, level to level, through short, snarling rivers; Mooselookmeguntic to the Richardsons to Pond-in-the-River, and through Rapid River to Umbagog, whence they empty into the Androscoggin and begin the long southeasterly curve back to the ocean. I like to say their names, and I wish I could make you see them—long, lovely, lonely stretches of water, shut in by dark hills. The trees come down to the shore, the black growth of fir and pine and spruce streaked with the lighter green of maple and birch. There is nothing at all on the hills but forest, and nobody lives there but deer and bear and wildcats. The people keep close to the lakes, building their dwellings in narrow clearings they have made by pushing the trees a little way back from the water. Our own clearing is on the Rapid River, just below the Pond-in-the-River Dam; and because Rapid River is not navigable, being the swiftest river east of the Rockies—it drops a hundred and eighty-five feet in three miles, with no falls, which is some kind of a record. We amazingly, live on a road. It doesn't go anywhere. It's really a carry between two lakes, so it is sensibly called the Carry Road. It starts at Middle Dam, on the Lower Richardson, and roughly follows the course of the river five miles to Sunday Cove on Umbagog. Halfway along, between road and river, is Forest Lodge, the sole address on the Carry Road, and our home. Forest Lodge is in the woods.

There is nothing north or south of us but trees for so many miles that sometimes it scares me to think about it. But actually it consists of one cabin, one shack, one large house in the worst cracker-box style, and an assortment of lean-to's, woodsheds, work-shops, and what are euphemistically known as out-houses. These latter are necessary because we have no plumbing, and therefore no bathroom. We get our water from the river and from a spring up back in the woods. We do our bathing in washtubs in front of the kitchen stove, and for other uses of the bathroom, we resort to the out-houses. This is no great hardship in summer, but in winter, with the snow knee deep, the wind howling like a maniac up the river, and the thermometer crawling down to ten below zero, it is a supreme test of fortitude to leave the warmth of the fire and go plunging out into the cold, no matter how great the necessity. We like to think, however, that it builds character.

We Took to the Woods – Chapter 2
"A Maine Guide"

I am married to a Maine guide. Of course a guide has to be a good woodsman and a canoe-man and camp cook and emergency doctor, and the State of Maine ascertains that he is, before issuing him a license to guide. But he could never earn a living if he didn't also make the grade with the sports—same as dudes of the west—as "quite the character." He has to be laconic. He has to be picturesque. Maine guides have a legend of quaintness to uphold, and boy! do they uphold it. They're so quaint that they creak. They ought to be. They work hard enough at it.

Here's the Maine guide. He wears what amounts to a

uniform. It consists of a wool shirt, preferably plaid, nicely faded to soft, warm tones; dark pants, either plus-fours, or for some unknown reason, riding breeches; wool socks and the soleless, Indian-type moccasin, or high laced boots. He carries a bandana in his hip pocket and may or may not wear another knotted around his neck. But he must wear a battered felt hat, with a collection of salmon flies stuck in the band, and he must wear it with an air; and he must wear a hunting knife day and night; and he must look tough and efficient. If he has high cheek bones and tans easily, that is his good luck. He can then admit to part-Indian ancestry, accurately or not. Indian blood is an item highly esteemed by sports. Naturally he could do his work as well in mail-order slacks, or in a tuxedo, for that matter; but the sports wouldn't think so. Sports are funny.

"That fellow there," the sport is supposed to say, showing his vacation movies in his Westchester rumpus room, "was my quarter-breed guide. He's quite a character. Never had any education beyond the seventh grade, but I don't know anyone I'd rather spend a week alone with. That's the real test. He's a genuine natural philosopher. For instance, we were talking about the War and he said "—and I never thought of it this way before—." What the guide said he probably lifted from Shirer's book, but translated into Down East, it wouldn't be recognizable.

A few livid scars are a great asset to a guide. It doesn't matter how he got them. Maybe as a barefoot boy he stepped on a rake. The holes make swell bear-trap scars, acquired one night up in the Allagash, when the thermometer was at thirty below and the nearest settlement was fifty miles away. Maybe he cut his hand peeling potatoes. It sounds much better to say that a beaver bit him. Maybe he fell down the stairs and gashed his forehead. When asked—and he'll be asked all right—he can tell all about his big fight with a lynx. They all make good stories to tell around the evening campfire.

Oh, those evening campfires! That's when the guide sows the seed for a re-engagement next year. This is the setup: for Supper—fresh caught trout with bacon curls, potatoes baked in the coals and slathered with butter, a kind of biscuit cooked in a frying pan and resembling Yorkshire pudding, canned peas and fruit. The sports, pleasantly stuffed and mildly weary from having "helped" paddle for ten or twelve miles, stretch out around the fire. Down on the shingle, that natural philosopher, that real character, Bobcat Bill, washes the dishes. The water glows like blood-stained ebony in the leaping light, and the firs stand up behind, black and motionless. Back in the bush a fox barks and a deer crashes away from the scent of woodsmoke. All around lies the wilderness, dark and unknown and sinister. Inside the little pool of light is all that is left of the safe and familiar—the canoes drawn up on the shore, the piled packsacks and blanket rolls, the forms and faces of friends. A loon sends its lost-soul lament over the darkening water, and a shiver runs around the fire. Then Bobcat Bill strolls up from the lake, throws an armful of *dry-ki* onto the blaze, and begins tossing blankets toward the group. In the flash of a buck's tail the old magic begins to work. The tight little fire-hearted circle of fellowship is formed. We're all brothers here, united by our common cause against the power of the black beyond. We're all valiant, noble renegades from civilization's chafing bonds. We're dangerous and free.

The loon throws its blood-curdling cry against the

Facing page: Rapids in the Carrabassett River

mountains once more, and laughs its crazy laughter.

"Never hear one of them critters a-hollerin,'" Bobcat Bill drifts easily into his act, "but what it 'minds me of—one time I was lost up on them big caribou barrens across the lake. That's how I come by this here scar on my shoulder. Reason I was up in there, a feller had met foul play—."

We Took to the Woods – Chapter 9, excerpt

The poor Riches, we don't have plays and music and contact with sophisticated minds, and a round of social engagements. All we have are sun and wind and rain, and space in which to move and breathe. All we have are the forests, and the calm expanses of the lakes, and time to call our own. All we have are the hunting and fishing and the swimming, and each other.

We don't see pictures in famous galleries. But the other day, after a sleet storm that had coated the world with a sheath of ice, I saw a pine grosbeak in a little poplar tree. The setting sun slanted through a gap in the black wall of the forest, and held bird and tree in a celestial spot-light. Every twig turned to diamond encrusted-gold, and the red of the bird's breast glowed like a huge ruby as he fluffed his feathers in the wind. I could hardly believe it. I could only stand still and stare.

And then I repeated to myself something that I once learned in the hope that it would safeguard me from ever becoming hardened to beauty and wonder. I found it long ago, when I had to study Emerson:

> If the stars should appear one night in a thousand years, how men would believe and adore; and preserve for many generations the remembrance of the city of God which has been shown!

Aster

Facing page: Autumn view of Rangeley Lake

One chatterbox of the North Woods is the ubiquitous red squirrel

Winter at Sebasticook Lake, Newport

Southern Lakes Area, Auburn, Lewiston, Augusta, Waterville, Skowhegan, and Newport

From Sebago Lake to Kezar Lake to the Winthrop, China, and Belgrade Lakes, and all the ponds and rivers in between, this area provides pleasurable summer resort towns and old historic villages located on the banks of clear blue lakes, ponds, and rivers. Yet on the Kennebec River of yesteryear, a great industry of ice-harvesting helped communities maintain economic viability after the woods had been cut down and the huge log drives via the rivers had ended. The tanning capability of the area led to shoe making, which still provides employment for many Mainers. Such old manufacturing towns like Skowhegan, Lewiston, Augusta, and Waterville, with its excellent and beautiful Colby College, were built among the farms and, while Mainers did not grow wealthy, they did not starve either. Lovely historic towns like Bethel, Waterford, Wayne, and Richmond tell of other times reflecting older architecture and gracious living. Augusta sits on the banks of the mighty Kennebec River and is the capitol of Maine. Its statehouse gazes down on old Fort Western, built as a defense against Native American uprisings in the 1750s.

Newport stream in winter

Bangor, Old Town, Orono, and Brewer

Bangor is an old manufacturing town on the Penobscot River. Stephen King winters here. Orono, just north of Bangor, is home to the University of Maine Black Bears and a first-class art museum. Nearby is Old Town, where Fort Knox is located and the famous Old Town canoes are built. At the northern tip of Old Town on the Penobscot River is Indian Island, home to the Penobscot Indian Reservation.

Chain of Lakes, Rangeley, Grafton Notch, Carrabassett River, and Chain-of-Ponds

The glamour of the Great North Woods resides here. Moose, deer, loons, and bear are easily seen, as accessibility via good roads and accommodations allow one to experience Maine's wilderness. The heart of this region follows a series of lakes and rivers: Aziscohos, Cupsuptic, Rangeley, Mooselookmeguntic, the upper and lower Richardsons, and Umbagog; and the Androscoggin, Rapid, and Sandy rivers, which flow into the Kennebec River. From Grafton Notch and its Screw Augur Falls to Wilsons Mills and beautiful Oquossoc and from gorgeous Rangeley to Stratton and historic Kingfield on the rapid Carrabassett River, this entire area is one of enchantment. Travelers can ski at Sugarloaf or Snow Mountain, snowmobile on a well laid out pattern of trails leading into Canada, hike on the Appalachian Trail, stop along the road to capture the vistas of Chain-of-Ponds northwest of Stratton, rent a boat at South Arm to travel to Lakewood Camp and walk the Carry Road. Louise Dickinson Rich lived here while she

Bateaux at Leonards Mills

The Gingerbread House Restaurant in Oquossoc

Facing page: Hawkweed blooms at a cemetery in Rangeley

penned her wonderful books of the North Woods. Near Kingfield is New Portland, which has an old wire suspension bridge that is unique and picturesque. Drive over it and one can feel its undulation. For those who love the woods, mountains, and lakes, I cannot think of a more beautiful region to visit.

Above right: A home in North Waterford

Below right: The old suspension bridge in New Portland

Below: A camp at South Arm, Lower Richardson Lake

*Screw Augur Falls,
Grafton Notch State Park*

Moosehead Lake, Greenville, Mount Kineo, Jackman, Moxie Falls, Dover-Foxcroft, Brownville

Here in the wild Great North Woods, paved roads travel great distances between villages while beyond these roads there are logging roads of dirt with no houses or services. In this particular area of Maine, Moosehead Lake, with its beautiful landmark of Mount Kineo and the Kennebeck River, holds court. There is a special campground, Lily Bay State Park, on the eastern shore. From Greenville on the south shore, the steamship, *The Katahdin*, provides tours around this magnificent lake. Jackman, a logging town, is located in the western part of this area, near the border of Canada and Quebec, and south of Jackman is West Forks, which is near the grand Moxie Falls. Southeast of Moosehead Lake and Greenville is Brownville Junction, home to Katahdin Ironworks, which owns a great deal of land here and, for a fee, will grant access to Gulf Hagus, a beautiful rock canyon that can be reached by a rugged four-mile trail.

Baxter State Park, Mount Katahdin, Millinocket, Ripogenus Dam, Allagash Wilderness Waterway

Baxter State Park is large and it is home to Maine's largest mountain, the 5,267-foot Mount Katahdin, terminal point of the long Appalachian Trail which winds its way north from the state of Georgia. One of the prettiest approaches to Mount Katahdin is from Moosehead Lake,

Facing page: Rangeley Lake house in winter

Mount Kineo, Moosehead Lake

The Great North Woods

Barn in Jackman

Spencer Pond Camps, Greenville

Facing page: Moosehead Lake at Rockwood

The Great North Woods

though much of this is dirt road. A remarkable gorge can be viewed from the Ripogenus Dam. Baxter State Park is at its loveliest in the fall with its colorful forest and shimmering blue ponds and lakes, and many hikers and mountain climbers relish the climbs and descents in this park. For the ultimate wilderness adventure, however, the magnificent Allagash Wilderness Waterway provides the most remote and nature-oriented canoeing opportunity in the east. From lake to river, one paddles a canoe north for 92 miles, without ever seeing one human resident. It is a memorable adventure for the most hardy.

Ferns on a riverbank

Facing page: Mount Katahdin from the West Branch of the Penobscot River

Ripogenus Gorge

Maine: A Portrait

Birch-shrouded drive in Baxter State Park

Aroostook County, Fort Kent, Madawaska, St. Johns River, Caribou, Presque Isle, and Houlton

Wooded and wild, man is but a visitor in most of Aroostook County. Only two main roads travel north and south along the Maine Woods, which are occasionally broken up by farms and traditional Maine logging and agriculture towns, such as Madawaska, Caribou, Presque Isle, Houlton, and Fort Kent, the terminus of US 1, which runs south all the way to Key West, Florida.

Old barn in Weston

Leaking-boot fountain in Houlton

Traditional working team and sledge, now used for recreation

The Great North Woods

Antique hayrake and cutter

Barn in a potato field, Monticello

Logging north of Rangeley

Afterword

Capt. Adam Bradford with a mussel harvest

This is an interpretation of Maine, the premise of which is that the environment has molded human endeavor to its own tempo. The changing nature of the weather and the northern latitude, the black flies and mosquitoes, and the Great North Woods with its river and lake corridors, have created an environment that some men can and have adjusted to. They enjoy a life of quiet independence, reflection, dignity, and simplicity. Despite its demands, they commune with the natural order and its commanding presence, and derive immense satisfaction from this. The sea, too, demands much of the fisherman—sometimes even his life. Maine is an environment that does not brook easily. It has little tolerance for idle chatter, weak constitutions, or fools. It demands individuals who are strong and respectful, with values based on living in harmony with the land, one's fellowman, and nature.

As the population and cities grow, nature is pushed back—in the air, on land, as well as at sea—until some line is crossed and man overpowers nature. When this happens, the lessons that the natural order teach us to balance both its and our survival will no longer have meaning, and we will be on a one-way course, with ever-increasing velocity, toward an environmental disaster of which the outcome is unknown. Maine is such a bellwether state and environment. May its leaders and people know this well, and continue to keep this state the gem that it is.

Donald Duncan, of the Duncan Clan, Boothbay

Lobster boat unloading in Southwest Harbor

Retired lobster boat, outside Castine

Afterword

Sizing up the haul, Stonington

A barnacle-encrusted buoy on Vinalhaven

Traps in Bernard

Gassing up, Southwest Harbor

Facing page: Stonington lobster pound

Maine: A Portrait

Above: Rocks shaped by wave action, Grindstone Point

Left: Sand Beach, Acadia National Park

Maine: A Portrait

Tidal pool with iris, grass, and rocks, Schoodic Point

Tidal pool at Acadia National Park

Following page: Tidal flats, South Trescott